Examining Health Care
What's the Public's Prescription?

Introduction   **2**

The U.S. spends more than any other country in the world on health care — $1.3 trillion in 2000, or $4,637 on every man, woman, and child. Yet serious problems with access, cost and quality persist, depriving many people of the care they need and jeopardizing the health of our nation.

From doctors to insurance executives, from patients to officeholders, an overwhelming number of Americans say we desperately need to reform health care in this country. But what is the best prescription for breaking down the barriers preventing so many people from receiving appropriate medical care?

At the heart of people's concerns about health care are important questions about what we value as Americans and what we are and are not willing to do to improve health care. Although they are not mutually exclusive, the following approaches reflect different perspectives and priorities that people bring to this critical issue.

Approach 1   **Connected Parts, Not Fragmented Pieces**   **8**

The most effective way to improve health care in America is to take firm hold of it and make it run like a true, well-coordinated system. We need to take the existing, unwieldy collection of health care fragments and fashion them into a connected web of health care services, where information flows readily between the pieces and they work in concert. This is the best way to curb costs and provide health care in a timely way.

Approach 2   **Partners, Not Just Patients**   **13**

We need to create new relationships in health care where consumers and professionals work hand-in-hand, with people becoming partners in their health care. We need to take time to communicate, to help people make informed decisions, and to educate for healthy lifestyles. This is the best way to improve the health of Americans and to lay a firm foundation for personal responsibility and prevention that will result in long-term savings.

Approach 3   **Care for All, Not Just for Some**   **18**

We need to set new priorities in health care aimed at providing Americans the care they need when they need it. We need to seal up the cracks in the system so that people don't fall through. We need an unflagging commitment providing the medical tre needs. This is the best way to improve individual health and prevent ill difficult and expensive to treat.

```
D1379022
```

Learn More about Health Care in America   **23**

Comparing Approaches   **24**

What Are the National Issues Forums?   **26**

Post-Forum Questionnaire   **27**

Examining Health Care

What's the Public's Prescription?

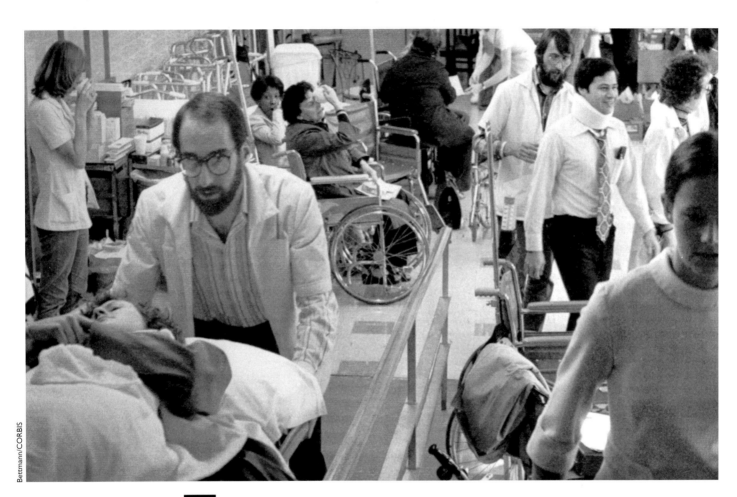

Bettmann/CORBIS

Crowded emergency rooms and shortages of medical professionals are straining many areas of the nation's health care system.

The United States is a nation of enormous wealth and resources with the highest standard of living in the world. Yet millions of Americans are not receiving the medical care they need to live in good health, and there is a widespread belief in the United States that the performance of our health care system is not nearly good enough.

A May 2002 survey by National Public Radio, the Kaiser Family Foundation, and Harvard's Kennedy School of Government found that 80 percent of Americans believe the health care system needs major changes or a complete rebuilding.

Troubling marks for U.S. health care come from health providers themselves. A recent survey by the Robert Wood Johnson Foundation found 58 percent of health care providers graded the health care system as "not very good."

Even more disturbing is the country's ranking on fairness and access for all. According to the World Health Organization, the U.S. ranks 54th out of 191 health care systems around the world.

The public's diagnosis

But the health care story cannot be told by just statistics and surveys. It is a story told by Americans when they talk about the realities they face each day.

They recount stories about waiting for hours to see their doctors, who then have only a few minutes to pinpoint and treat their problems. When specialists are needed, referrals are subject to close scrutiny and potential denial by insurers. And while there is an abundance of information available about health care, people say they are not sure how to find it or which sources to trust.

People often describe the care they receive as fragmented and incomplete. When a person has several physicians, there may be no one provider taking responsibility for coordinating that care in a holistic way. In many cases, people lack access to certain services they view as essential to their health, such as preventive care, prescription drugs, and dental, vision, and mental health services.

In many parts of the country — urban and rural — there are shortages of doctors, nurses, and medical facilities. And many patients feel they have little say in their own fate. Crucial decisions about their lives are being made by administrators with cost efficiency charts instead of by patients and families consulting with doctors they know and trust.

The problems are compounded for more than 41 million Americans without health insurance. For many, their only option is a hospital emergency room. They rarely see the same doctor twice. They delay care to avoid bills they cannot afford. They may postpone care until their problems become critical and more difficult to treat.

Health care consumers are not alone in their discontent. Health providers say pressures to control cost undermine good patient care. Employers say they can't meet the ever-escalating costs of health insurance plans. Insurers struggle to come up with plans that provide an ever-expanding array of services at an affordable cost. Government agencies that fund care for the poor and elderly say tax dollars don't stretch far enough to meet the need.

At the same time, when Americans talk about health care, most say we benefit from well-trained doctors and nurses, the latest technological advances, new prescription medicines that save

> In many parts of the country — urban and rural — there are shortages of doctors, nurses, and medical facilities.

Getty Images

Senior citizens participate in a bus trip from Pennsylvania to Ontario, Canada, where they plan to purchase medications because of the difference in price.

lives, and insurance programs that cover the majority of people in the United States. This makes it all the more frustrating and often heartbreaking, that so many people are not getting appropriate medical care. To most Americans, this is not acceptable, and they want to remedy it as quickly as possible. The question, of course, is how.

Many believe that, unless bold steps are taken, the condition of health care will only get worse. The aging of the baby boomers, economic downturns, and threats to public safety place additional demands on a health care system that is already stretched to — and some say beyond — its limits.

America's health: Good, but good enough?

"Americans on average are living longer than ever before, and much of this is due to the progress we've made in fighting diseases that account for the majority of deaths in the country," said Secretary Tommy Thompson of the U.S. Department of Health and Human Services when he released the preliminary data for 2000.

The declining death rates for heart disease and cancer are particularly encouraging. These diseases account for more than half of all deaths in the country each year. Heart disease death rates have been dropping steadily since 1950, and cancer death rates have been falling since 1990.

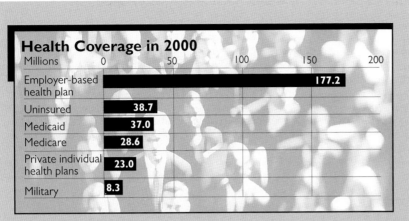

Health Coverage in 2000

Millions	0	50	100	150	200
Employer-based health plan					177.2
Uninsured	38.7				
Medicaid	37.0				
Medicare	28.6				
Private individual health plans	23.0				
Military	8.3				

Source: U.S. Census Bureau

The largest source of health coverage in the United States is employer-sponsored plans, which cover almost two-thirds (64.1 percent) of Americans. The next largest source is Medicaid, which funds care for low-income people with state taxes matched by federal funds. The third largest source of health coverage is Medicare, which funds care to elderly and disabled persons and is financed largely by federal payroll taxes.

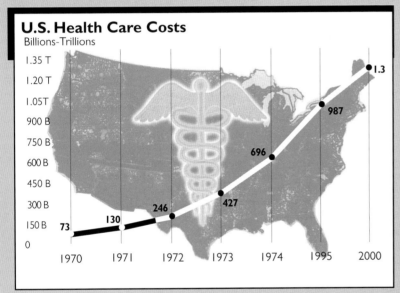

U.S. Health Care Costs

Billions-Trillions

1.35 T	
1.20 T	1.3
1.05T	
900 B	987
750 B	
600 B	696
450 B	
300 B	427
150 B	73 130 246
0	
	1970 1971 1972 1973 1974 1995 2000

Source: Centers for Disease Control and Prevention

Death rates for AIDS have dropped for five straight years.

While American health in general appears to be improving all the time, is it good enough? The U.S. spends more than any other country in the world on health care — $1.3 trillion in 2000, or $4,637 on every man, woman, and child. Even though we are improving, we still lag behind much of the industrialized world in the key indicators of life expectancy and infant mortality.

The changing health care system

The way we deliver health care has changed dramatically during the last two decades. Six of ten surgeries are now performed on an outpatient basis, up by three-quarters over the last 15 years. People are admitted to hospitals less often and their stays are shorter. Advances in pharmaceutical research have created new treatment options, and the number of prescriptions dispensed per person has increased by nearly 50 percent since 1994.

The way we make health care decisions also has changed. Nine of ten Americans who are insured through their employers are in some type of managed care plan, a type of insurance requiring a person to choose a primary care physician for most ailments. These primary doctors can then refer patients to specialists, if needed. Proponents of managed care say it provides quality care and, at the same time, keeps down health care costs.

But many Americans have concerns about managed care and the insurance industry in general. A poll conducted for the W.K. Kellogg Foundation found about two-thirds of Americans say patients should have the biggest say in decisions about their health care, but only about one-fifth felt they actually do. Another poll done for the Kaiser Family Foundation found that although most people with private health insurance were basically satisfied with their health plans, more than half worried that if they became sick their health plan would be more concerned about saving money than providing the best treatment for them.

Multiple health care ills

Perhaps the most daunting aspect of improving health care is that so many aspects of it seem to be in trouble. Virtually every type of person involved with health care is calling for some kind of reform, and concerns cover everything from quality, to communication, to cost, to lack of coordination, to who has access and who does not.

A short list of compelling challenges shows the range and complexity of the issue:

■ **Lack of insurance.** For many people, the main concern is not the quality of care they receive, but whether or not they are able to obtain care at all. Almost 14 percent of the U.S. population had no health insurance for the entire year of 2000.

Medicaid does indeed provide coverage for the nation's poorest people, although eligibility and services vary from state to state. At the other end of the income scale, highly paid workers almost always have access to insurance through their employers and can afford the premiums. The majority of the uninsured are those in the middle — people who work in jobs where they earn too much to qualify for Medicaid, but not enough to afford insurance. More than 80 percent of uninsured children and adults under age 65 live in families where at least one person is employed.

In May 2002, in an analysis of 130 studies on the effects of not having health insurance, the National Academy of Sciences concluded that through delayed diagnoses and increased complications, lack of insurance leads to 18,000 premature deaths each year. This figure includes 1,400 early deaths due to high blood pressure, 1,200 to 1,400 early deaths among HIV-infected adults, and 360 to 600 premature deaths from breast cancer. Reed Tuckson, a senior vice president of the United Health Group and member of the report committee, called the findings "a major American problem" and a "tragedy of numbers."

Such figures should be seen in the context of today's sagging economy, which has increased the number of unemployed by 2 million and reduced company health benefits to employees and retirees because of rising medical costs. Legislatures in dozens of states have similarly cut funds for Medicaid.

■ **Rising costs.** Escalating health care costs are a concern to all Americans, whether they have insurance or not. Managed care plans helped slow health insurance price increases

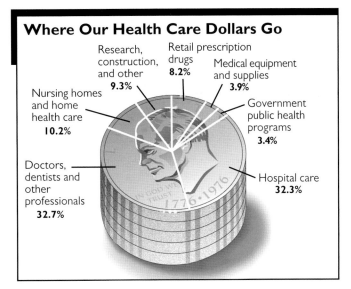

Where Our Health Care Dollars Go

- Research, construction, and other **9.3%**
- Retail prescription drugs **8.2%**
- Medical equipment and supplies **3.9%**
- Nursing homes and home health care **10.2%**
- Government public health programs **3.4%**
- Doctors, dentists and other professionals **32.7%**
- Hospital care **32.3%**

Source: Centers for Disease Control and Prevention

during the mid 1990s, but costs have since returned to the double-digit inflation of the 1980s. Nationally, private health insurance premiums rose an average of 12 percent in 2001 and are expected to rise another 15 percent in 2002.

Insurers point out that in the early 1990s the "managed care" philosophy of health maintenance organizations succeeded in lowering and containing medical costs. But today, like other health insurers, health maintenance organizations are caught on a wave of rising prices and are struggling to stay afloat, especially when the public desires an ever-expanding array of services. In recent years, some HMOs have refused to accept

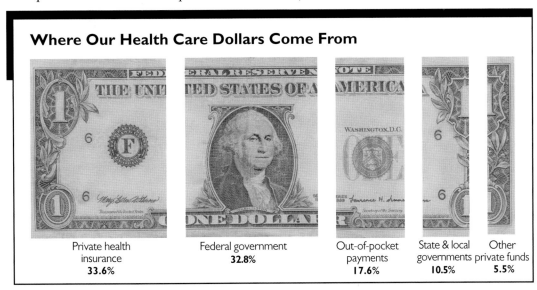

Where Our Health Care Dollars Come From

Private health insurance	Federal government	Out-of-pocket payments	State & local governments	Other private funds
33.6%	**32.8%**	**17.6%**	**10.5%**	**5.5%**

Source: Centers for Disease Control and Prevention

AP/Wide World Photos

Members of the public watch as the House Judiciary Committee in Jackson, Mississippi, considers rule changes for medical malpractice lawsuits.

and other rising costs, some doctors, particularly those in specialties most subject to lawsuits, are finding it difficult to keep their practices open. Many obstetricians have stopped delivering babies and have limited their practice to gynecology because their insurance premiums have become too expensive, making it more difficult for expectant mothers to find good pre-natal care.

■ **Troubling disparities.** Race and ethnicity affect the quality of care people receive. Even when income and insurance status are comparable, racial and ethnic minorities receive lower-quality care than whites do, according to a large volume of studies. Minorities are less likely to get the most appropriate heart medications or bypass surgery, cancer tests and treatments, or HIV drugs. They are more likely, on the other hand, to receive less-desirable procedures, such as lower-limb amputations for diabetes.

Although life expectancy is edging upward for all racial groups, racial minorities still lag behind. The death rate for black Americans is a third higher than that of white Americans. Infant mortality rates are significantly higher for babies of black and American Indian mothers.

people on Medicare because, they claim, the fees allowed by the U.S. government are insufficient to cover their costs.

In June 2002, Families USA, a consumer group, reported the prices of the top 50 most-prescribed drugs nearly tripled during the previous year. According to the Kaiser Family Foundation, prescription drugs accounted for nearly 20 percent of national expenditures in 1999-2000, up from 9 percent in 1993-1994. Drug prices have risen so steadily that at least 28 states are looking for legal remedies to force drug companies to lower their prices. By the spring of 2002, three federal court judgments sided with the states.

> Although life expectancy is edging upward for all racial groups, racial minorities still lag behind.

People with annual incomes under $7,500 are almost twice as likely to die prematurely as those making more than $32,500. Blacks and Hispanics are three times more likely to live in poverty than are whites.

■ **The baby boomer demands on Medicare.** Economists warn that Medicare's long-term financial survival is seriously threatened by the country's changing demographics. Not only will there be more beneficiaries as baby boomers retire, but there will also be fewer workers to support each retiree with their payments into the system. In the next decades, aging baby boomers will bring a mammoth challenge to Medicare, which even now is struggling to find the funds to help pay for prescription drugs.

■ **Shortages of medical facilities, personnel, and services.** In recent years more than 250 hospitals have closed because they could not support themselves. A large number of nurses are leaving their profession because of low pay and poor working conditions. Facing the high cost of malpractice insurance

David Walker, Comptroller General of the United States, says, "long-term simulations show a world by 2030 in which Social Security, Medicare, and Medicaid absorb most of the available revenues within the federal budget. Under this scenario, these programs would require more than three-quarters of total federal revenue, even without adding a Medicare prescription drug benefit. Without meaningful reform, demographic and cost trends will drive Medicare spending to unsustainable levels."

Health care in America: The public's prescription?

From doctors to insurance executives, from patients to officeholders, an overwhelming number of Americans say we desperately need to reform health care in this country. But what is the best prescription for breaking down the barriers preventing so many people from receiving appropriate medical care?

Careful thought and deliberation are needed to understand the nature of the problems in health care, their impact on people's health, and possible courses of action. These approaches are based on the broad and deep concerns expressed by Americans.

Approach One: Some say the surest and best treatment is to overhaul the system so it runs like a well-coordinated, well-managed web of connected services.

Approach Two: Others say the true remedy is to fundamentally improve the relationship between doctors and patients, by giving people the responsibility of being true partners in their health care.

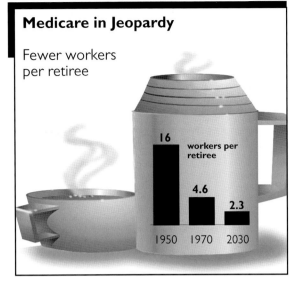

Medicare in Jeopardy

Fewer workers per retiree

16 / workers per retiree

4.6

2.3

1950 1970 2030

Source: Centers for Disease Control and Prevention

Approach Three: Still others say the best medicine is a new and higher commitment to ensuring that all Americans get the care necessary for them to be in good health.

While these approaches are not mutually exclusive, they do reflect different perspectives and priorities about what should be done to improve health care in America. This discussion guide examines these three approaches, looking at the benefits and drawbacks of each, the actions we would take and the tradeoffs we would have to accept. It is intended to help all of us talk together in groups large and small, deliberate together, and consider what directions we should take.

"Unfortunately, you have what we call 'no insurance.'"

Connected Parts, Not Fragmented Pieces

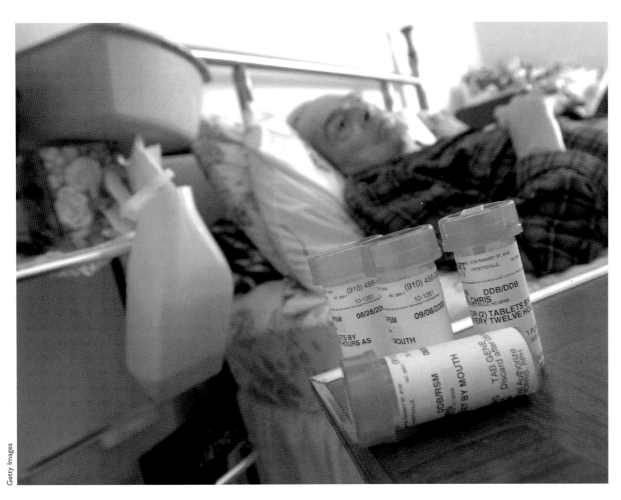

Getty Images

Many patients, like this man from Fayetteville, North Carolina, must carefully monitor the interactions of multiple medications.

"We almost lost my father-in-law a few years ago," says a registered nurse in West Virginia. "When he was in the hospital, he had six different doctors and was on eight different medications. They were all good doctors and they all did their part, but I still stayed with him as much as I could to make sure all the parts got connected. When one of his doctors decided to step in to coordinate all the treatments and services, it was a huge relief. And I think it made the difference in bringing him back to health. But not everyone has a nurse in the family or a physician willing to work so hard to connect the dots."

Many people worry that health care in America is out of control, that no one is responsible for overseeing or coordinating all the various parts of the system. At a personal level, patients often feel that they're farmed out to different specialists with no one paying attention to the big picture.

We call our current method of delivering health care in the United States "a system," but that's giving it too much credit, according to Approach One. It is often chaotic and disjointed, with each of its many hands not knowing what the others are doing. Organizations and agencies that provide medical care do not coordinate their services. Some clinics in a community serve few people, while others overflow. The American Hospital Association says that one-third of all emergency rooms are so crowded that ambulances are diverted to other hospitals. Different clinicians who treat a patient for various ailments do not pass information back and forth.

The quality of care is jeopardized daily by troubling problems such as ever-rising costs, shortages of doctors and nurses, waste, fraud, and medical mistakes — all symptoms of a system that lacks coordination and controls. What we have, according to Approach One, is not a health care system at all but a disorganized and expanding assortment of elements — hospitals, insurance companies, researchers, medical schools, health professionals, pharmaceutical companies — each one dealing with its own immediate task.

What Can Be Done?

- Citizens and professionals could serve on health care councils which coordinate the use of facilities and medical services within a region.
- Health care providers could develop systems to share patient information and coordinate care.
- Patients could make sure their doctors are aware of treatments from other doctors and could carry a "health passport" card containing their medical history.
- Insurers could set guidelines to reduce unnecessary medical tests, and medical schools could educate physicians to use costly procedures efficiently.
- Legislators could enact laws to increase the monitoring of health care billing practices and stiffen penalties for fraud.
- Congress could establish a nationwide mandatory reporting system to monitor and learn from medical errors.
- Hospitals could limit the use of emergency rooms to emergency care only.
- Legislators could set caps on awards for medical lawsuits.

Approach One says that, even with everyone's best individual efforts, the overall needs of the patient are not being met. A well-run, well-coordinated web of health care services is the best way to significantly curb costs and give people sound medical treatment in a timely way. And it is

AP/Wide World Photos

Patients sit in the waiting room of the Bell Gardens Health Center in Los Angeles, one of nine public health clinics in the county that closed their doors recently, victims of budget cuts.

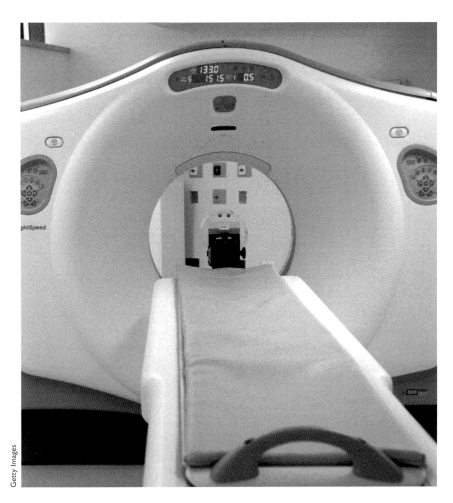

Getty Images

Expensive high-speed Cat Scans are widely recognized as an important advancement in medical diagnostics.

improve care and minimize both organizations' health care costs. The military health system is expected to take about $20 billion of the federal budget in 2003.

"As we face the threat of terrorism, it is more important than ever that we ensure effective coordination and cooperation with other federal agencies and organizations with necessary expertise," Dr. Bill Winkenwerder, the assistant secretary of defense for health affairs, said in prepared remarks to Congress. Winkenwerder said the two agencies could work together through exchanging information, examining ways to jointly purchase medicine, establishing solid business procedures for reimbursements, and joining for long-range planning.

Passport to better health

Signs of increased coordination are springing up in many areas of heath care.

One experiment in three western states aims to coordinate information and eliminate the paper work burdening patients any time they see another doctor, or move, or seek insurance and must obtain files, x-rays, and permissions.

Nevada, North Dakota, and Wyoming are testing a Health Passport Card, a small personal document the same size as a credit card. The card contains essential information about a person's medical history, medications, prescriptions, health insurance coverage, and other related information, including participation in government programs like Medicaid, WIC, and Head Start. It accesses Internet-based accounts of personal medical information. It can be used at doctor's offices, clinics, hospitals, and other places where information on a patient might be needed instantaneously.

The three states have distributed thousands of cards that are being used for a limited number of services. If these "smart" health cards prove successful, the experiment will reach out to include more people and more services. Advocates of increased coordination point to the Health Passport as an example of how coordination can save time and energy and, more importantly, enable prompt and accurate assessment of health care needs.

the best route to fairness in delivering good care because it uses resources where they can do the most good.

The need for coordination

Much of the way we currently do business is built on assumptions that competition between hospitals, between insurers, and between pharmaceutical companies keeps costs in check and quality high.

Approach One says that this system simply is not working when it comes to health care, so we must do what is necessary to clear that hurdle. Health providers must begin cooperating and coordinating their services, for the good of public health. In some parts of the country, local and regional health care councils are devising plans to share equipment and supplies and to coordinate medical services and the use of facilities.

It's not just in civilian life where cooperation and close coordination of resources make sense. In March 2002, the Defense Department said it is looking to build "a mutually beneficial partnership" with the Department of Veterans Affairs to

The high cost of waste and fraud

Many people are concerned that American health care is terribly wasteful, with patients demanding services they don't truly need and doctors ordering unnecessary tests to protect themselves against lawsuits. In addition, people say the sheer size and complexity of the health care system make it ripe for fraud and abuse. Health care fraud costs were an estimated $54 billion in 1997, according to the Coalition Against Insurance Fraud. The amount was more than the entire nation spent on dental care that year.

Minimizing waste in the system is not just being advocated by watchdog organizations and consumer groups, but by businesses, such as General Motors, the largest private purchaser of health care in the United States. GM is part of the Leapfrog Group, a national employers' movement trying to instigate health care improvements. James Cubbins, GM's executive director of its health care initiatives, estimates as much as 30 percent of health care costs are waste.

Some cases of fraud result from over billing by health care providers. Undercover investigators attended workshops conducted by consultants on how health providers can "run a more profitable practice" and "audit-proof" their practices. The consultants' advice included not reporting overpayments made by insurance carriers, performing tests not medically necessary to beef up documentation, and limiting services provided to people with low-paying insurance plans. The investigators found some of the advice violated federal rules.

Other cases reveal clearly criminal intent. Investigators have uncovered "rent-a-patient" operations in which phony health providers hire people to bring patients to their "clinics," where they provide cursory services. They then bill Medicaid, Medicare, and private insurance for services that often were not provided.

In another illegal scheme investigators call the "pill mill," patients are given prescriptions they don't need, which they have filled and then sell back to middlemen, who sell them back to pharmacies. The pills are repeatedly dispensed and billed to insurers and may eventually be dispersed to legitimate patients.

Waste and fraud deprive the health care system of much-needed funds that could provide high-quality health care to more Americans, according to Approach One. We must make sure that medical bills are monitored to catch errors and overbilling, and that stiffer penalties are imposed for health care fraud.

Too many medical mistakes

In today's complex and fast-paced world of health care, the potential for medical errors exists in every practice, every day. Such errors include wrong or conflicting medications, surgical mistakes, falls, and mistaken patient identities.

> **Every year, at least 44,000 Americans die from preventable medical errors.**
>
> — The Institute of Medicine of the National Academies of Science

Every year, at least 44,000 Americans die from preventable medical errors, according to a report by the Institute of Medicine of the National Academies of Science. The financial toll of these errors, including the cost of additional care, lost income, and disability, is at least $17 billion.

Studies have found that these mistakes are not so much related to individual incompetence or recklessness as they are to basic flaws in how the health care system is organized. For example, when a person is treated by multiple health providers, the providers may lack critical information about how each is treating the patient and end up providing conflicting — and sometimes deadly — treatments.

"These stunningly high rates of medical errors — resulting in deaths, permanent disability, and unnecessary suffering — are simply unacceptable in a medical system that first promises to 'do no harm,'" says William Richardson, president

Photos of thousands of babies delivered by doctors in Henderson, Nevada, hang on the wall of the Women's Wellness Center. The clinic has turned away patients recently, citing the rising cost of malpractice insurance.

AP/Wide World Photos

What Costs and Tradeoffs Should We Be Prepared to Accept ?

A Likely Tradeoff

- This approach uses scarce health care resources to develop systems for coordinating medical care, rather than providing direct care to patients.

Concerns about This Approach

- Increased legislation adds extra layers to a health care system already choked by bureaucracy.
- Making personal medical records more available makes personal privacy more vulnerable.
- Limiting malpractice awards constrains citizens' rights for appropriate compensation.
- Focusing on medical errors casts doubt on the vast majority of medical professionals who are highly skilled and competent.

of the W.K. Kellogg Foundation and chair of the committee that wrote the report. "Our recommendations are intended to encourage the health care system to take the actions necessary to improve safety. We must have a health care system that makes it easy to do things right and hard to do them wrong."

We must do everything we can to prevent mistakes in health care, according to Approach One. This means putting in place a better system for doctors and other providers of health care to share information so that treatments for each patient are well coordinated and don't conflict. And it means monitoring and learning from medical mistakes, which must start with errors being reported by all involved.

The malpractice dilemma

While unintentional medical errors can be tragic, this approach says we also need to confront and control the chilling effect of large malpractice awards against doctors, hospitals, and their insurance companies. Such lawsuits stand in the way of health care in America working as it should, with everyone seeking the same goal of excellence in patient care.

Across the nation, a terrible toll is being taken in the number of physicians who "have been forced to discontinue high-risk procedures, leave their stand and retire early because of out-of-control legal climates and skyrocketing liability

premiums," according to Richard F. Corlin, president of the American Medical Association. The AMA is lobbying hard for changes in malpractice and medical liability practices, pointing to facts such as a 30 percent increase in insurance rates to doctors in eight states in 2001.

Dr. Corlin also cites glaring examples such as malpractice insurance rates as high as $203,000 for some obstetricians in Florida and $134,000 for some surgeons in Texas. The AMA argues that we need to bring "common sense" back to the system of insurance for physicians. And Corlin cites a recent study by the Health Care Liability Alliance that says 78 percent of Americans surveyed are concerned about the effects of rising insurance costs for health care providers, and 73 percent favor laws that limit awards for "pain and suffering."

Across the country, obstetricians in particular are watching their medical malpractice premiums soar. In Mississippi, Dr. Scott Nelson stopped delivering babies after his annual malpractice insurance premium topped $100,000. For the last six years, Mississippi juries have awarded unprecedented numbers of malpractice awards of more than $1 million per incident. The number of practicing obstetricians in Nelson's region has dropped from six to three.

"Patients are going to have to wait longer to see doctors," Nelson told *American Medical News.* "The doctors that are left right now are going to have an excessive load. I'm standing ready, willing, and able in a part of the country that is underserved, and I can't provide care because I can't afford the insurance. We've got a real mess on our hands."

Most doctors are finding ways to pay for insurance, but many are keenly aware of trends with medical lawsuits, causing them to protect themselves by ordering extra or unnecessary tests, as well as sending patients to specialists to confirm their diagnosis and spread around the responsibility for treatment. Many say the most profound effect of curbing awards in medical lawsuits would be to save untold millions of dollars in wasteful and unnecessary tests and extra visits to doctors' offices. Those resources need to be spent to improve the overall quality of health care in America.

Partners, Not Just Patients

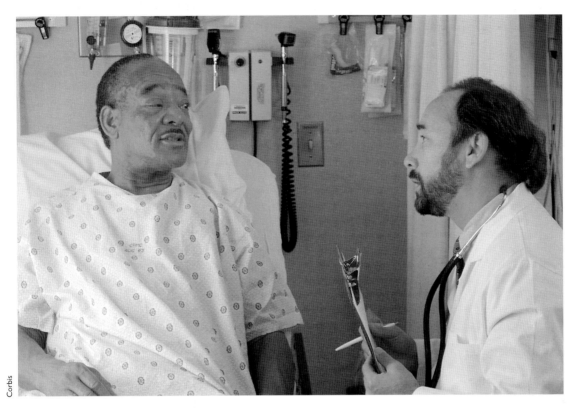

Corbis

Many patients and physicians report improved quality of health care when increased time is spent discussing health concerns, illnesses, and treatments.

"**H**ealth care appears to be evolving into more of a commercial endeavor than a service to the human condition," says a South Dakota physician. "Technology has allowed for great medical treatments, but at a cost that is alienating people from its benefits."

"There is a huge distinction between health services and health care," a woman from Georgia agrees. "I seek health care, but sometimes have to settle for health services. I want to be a partner in my health care and share the responsibility with my doctors and nurses."

How individuals are treated — personally, as well as medically — has a significant effect on their ability to heal and stay well. People want relationships with health professionals they know and trust. They want their providers to listen to their concerns, discuss their options, and honor their choices.

In this view, the patient-doctor relationship has always been and will always be at the heart of quality health care. No matter how we pay for medical care, or how it is managed and coordinated, or how many people lend a helping hand, it cannot improve significantly until patients and their doctors refashion their relationship and put patients at the center of health care decisions.

The best way to improve health care in America is by creating new relationships in which patients are partners, according to Approach Two. This means taking time to communicate, honoring individual differences, helping people make informed decisions, educating for healthy lifestyles, respecting individual rights and expecting individual responsibility. We need to create new relationships where health care consumers and medical professionals work hand in hand.

What Can Be Done

- Insurers and health care administrators could support more face-to-face time between doctors and patients.
- Medical school training could focus on doctor-patient collaboration and "patient-centered care."
- Media and schools could provide more information about health risks, such as smoking and obesity.
- Citizens could serve on medical licensing, review, and health assistance boards.
- Employers could involve employees in decisions about health plans, benefits, and costs.
- Individuals could take more responsibility for practicing healthy habits and preventive health care.
- Insurers could charge higher premiums to customers who engage in risky health habits.
- Legislators could pass laws to protect patients' rights to appeal decisions by insurers.
- Community groups could provide health education and opportunities to discuss public health care policies.

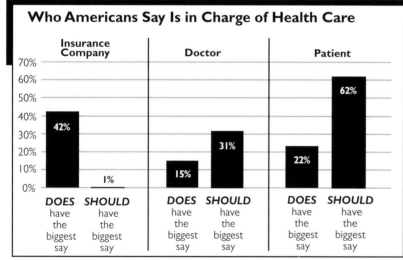

Source: W.K. Kellogg Foundation

Patient-centered care

Putting patients at the center of their own health care is not a new concept. But a growing number of studies is showing that greater involvement of patients in determining their care leads to improved health. Evidence of improving health care keeps stacking up behind the concepts of "patient-centered care."

The National Institute of Mental Health defines patient-centered care as "health care that establishes a partnership among practitioners,

patients, and their families (when appropriate) to ensure that decisions respect patients' wants, needs, and preferences and solicit patients' input on the education and support they need to make decisions and participate in their own care." In 2001, the institute announced that, according to their research, patients who are "active participants" in their care experience better results than those who are not.

The National Academies of Science has studied in depth the need for reforming health care in America. Published in 2002, its *Rules for Health Care Reform,* put forth recommendations for improving health care for patients by customizing it to individual needs, accommodating increased choice and control over their own care, and sharing information openly.

This approach enables professionals and patients to discuss the substantial effects that behavior can have on health, both good and bad. Writing in the May 2002 issue of the *American Journal of Preventive Medicine,* Evelyn Whitlock observes that doctor-patient collaboration could be a powerful weapon against half the causes of death in the United States. Whitlock, a senior investigator at the Kaiser Permanente Center for Health Research, argues that through working cooperatively with patients, clinicians can help patients break destructive behavior and adopt a healthier lifestyle.

Time to build trust

"Doctor, listen to me," is a Michigan woman's message. "Talk to me and listen to what I'm saying. And it may not be just the ailment I'm coming in with today, but something that happened last week that caused it, and I'm not making that connection."

Across America, people say they want more time with their health providers to ask questions, get information, and weigh their alternatives. "When there are relationships and true caring, health problems are more easily resolved," says a Georgia doctor. "Trust is key. You must have a relationship with the people who provide your care. Care and relationships take time."

"A patient may need time to talk," a North Carolina nurse agrees. "There are a lot of emotions that go into a person's illness. When people don't know what's going to happen, they become very anxious. For us to be able to ease some of that anxiety is a key part of what we do."

But time is a scarce resource in today's health

care environment. "I see it as an ethical dilemma for the physicians," says one health care administrator. "The physicians want to take care of people. They have been trained to take care of people. They want to serve the underserved. But they also want to have a reasonable income compatible with their geographical area. And to do this, they've got to see more patients, see them quicker, see them more efficiently, and do it for less."

Trusting relationships are the foundation of effective health care, according to Approach Two, and these take time to build. This means providing more one-on-one time between patients and their doctors, nurses, and other medical professionals. And it means making sure that insurance plans cover this consultation time.

Respect cultural differences

Some people say they have problems getting appropriate care from health providers who do not understand and respect their cultural beliefs. American Indians, for instance, often encounter difficulties when their traditions are not recognized or supported by the health care system.

"Most often when someone is ill we want to visit as a family," says a Lakota woman. "This family support is critical, especially when a relative may be surrounded by a system that feels cold and clinical. However, most hospitals don't want a large group in a room, particularly if that group includes children and babies. They do not welcome us and often ban groups in ways both subtle and not so subtle."

Recent immigrants say that language is a barrier to getting effective care. Nearly 14 million Americans do not speak English proficiently, and many communities with large immigrant popluations don't have enough trained medical interpreters.

"I was in the doctor's office, and no one could explain to me what the doctor tried to tell me," says a Hispanic immigrant in Florida. "The only thing I said was 'okay' when he asked me if I understood. But, really, I did not understand. Now I don't have that problem because I've learned English. But there are a lot of communities that don't speak English, and they need help."

Health care in America must take into account the diverse cultural and medical priorities of its people, according to Approach Two. This means making physicians and other clinicians aware of those differences so that they can appropriately care for everyone who seeks treatment.

Need for reliable information

Across the country, people say they need reliable information in order to make good choices about health care services and providers. From delivering babies to end-of-life care, people want to know their options and the benefits and risks of each. Groups such as Healthwise, Inc., translate confusing medical jargon into terms that lay people can understand. This nonprofit organization of health professionals publishes a wealth of information that advises consumers on diseases and their symptoms and when to consult a doctor.

People also want more information about the quality of the care given by health providers. Seven in ten people say that information about medical errors and malpractice suits would be the biggest help to them in determining the quality of health providers. They're also interested in knowing how much experience a doctor or hospital has in conducting particular tests and procedures.

Many people — especially young people — are turning to the Internet for advice. One survey found that more teens and young adults were going on-line for health information (75 percent) than they were to play games, participate in chat rooms, shop, or check sports scores. Disparities remain, however, in Internet use based on race and income. Only about half (55 percent) of Hispanic and two-thirds (66 percent) of black youth have Internet access from home, compared to 80 percent of white youth. Twice as many low-income youth (15 percent) have never been on-line as compared to high-income youth (7 percent).

Of course, the extensive medical information on the Internet and its use by such large numbers of individuals raises questions about the reliability of the information and the lure of self-diagnosis. A growing number of medical professionals see it as more important than ever that they provide patients with good information, both in their conversations with patients and in the written material they provide.

Getty Images

A woman practices yoga at the "Fun, Fit and Free Festival" in Philadelphia.

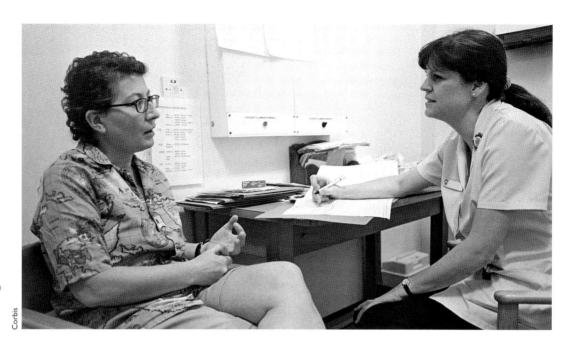

A patient and health care provider spend time discussing health concerns.

Corbis

As part of the drive for accurate information, health care consumers, employers, and others are forming groups like FACCT — the Foundation for Accountability — an organization that has developed measures of health care quality and publishes the information. FACCT describes itself as an organization that "believes that clear, relevant information about quality in the hands of consumers will lead to a health care market that delivers value and a health care system that improves health. With information about quality, consumers can make sound buying decisions, participate effectively in their own care, and encourage the health system to focus on health."

When armed with good information, people will make the health care decisions that are right for them, according to this view. This means that health organizations, medical professionals, and the media need to increase education about good preventive medicine, health risks, and proper treatment of ailments, and do so in a way that is clear and easy to understand.

The expertise of consumers

"Patient-centered outcomes have taken center stage as the primary means of measuring the effectiveness of health care," write Roger Bolus and Jennifer Pitts for *Managed Care* on-line magazine. "It is commonly acknowledged that patients' reports of their health, and quality of life and their satisfaction with the quality of care and services, are as important as many clinical health measures."

The "consumer movement" in health care offers health practitioners and policymakers valuable insights into how to make health care in America more efficient and effective. For example, Community Voices Miami (a local coalition) held 18 community dialogues on health care throughout Miami-Dade County, involving 700 people. The group issued a detailed report of the findings from the dialogues, which are now being used by health providers and planners to improve local health services.

Unhealthy Behaviors
% of Adults

Behavior	%
Binge drinking	14.9%
Smoking	23.2%
No leisure-time exercise	26.9%
Overweight or obese	56.8%

Source: Centers for Disease Control and Prevention

At the national level, a variety of groups have formed to bring the consumer perspective into public discussions about health care. Some groups like Families USA and Consumers Union have a broad focus on a variety of health care issues. Others have come together to give a voice to specific groups. Family Voices, for instance, was formed by a group of parents concerned about children with special health care needs. With a volunteer coordinator in every state, the group's 40,000 members work to improve health policy and practice at local, state, and national levels.

We must tap the expertise of both consumers and professionals to create a more responsive health care system in America, according to Approach Two. This means making sure that consumers are consulted and included in decision-making about health care, including serving along with health professionals on government, hospital, and employer boards that set health care policies.

A two-way street of rights and responsibilities

Since 1995, Congress has been considering legislation aimed at establishing minimum procedural protections for all Americans, regardless of the type of health plan they have. Commonly referred to as the "Patients' Bill of Rights," the law would establish requirements for clear disclosure of health plan rules, access to specialists and emergency care, and internal and external processes to review denials of care. But the legislation has been stalled by disagreement over patients' rights to sue their health plans and if so, what standards would apply.

Many Americans add that with rights come responsibilities. "Why should we pay for other people's bad health habits?" they ask, claiming that too many Americans are not doing their part. The human suffering and financial toll of many diseases could be avoided if more people made healthy lifestyle decisions. So could the demand on other precious resources, such as medicine, hospital rooms, and doctors' time.

> The human suffering and financial toll of many diseases could be avoided if more people made healthy lifestyle decisions.

What Costs and Tradeoffs Should We Be Prepared to Accept?

A Likely Tradeoff
- This approach depends on the time-consuming work of changing relationships and personal habits rather than addressing existing gaps in health coverage.

Concerns about This Approach
- Many people will not be willing or able to be so involved in learning about their illnesses and treatments.
- Demands for physicians' and nurses' time will strain a system that is already stretched too thin.
- Doctors should focus on practicing effective clinical treatments, not developing personal relationships.
- Shared decision-making confuses who is responsible for medical decisions and treatment.

For example, tobacco use is the single most preventable cause of death in the United States. The American Lung Association says that tobacco use accounts annually for about 430,000 deaths and costs an estimated $97.2 billion in health care expenditures and lost productivity.

Personal responsibility for health must begin at a young age. Smoking, for example, almost always begins during the teen years and the prevalence of teen smoking has increased over the past ten years. Nearly 3,000 minors begin smoking everyday. If current patterns continue, one-third of adolescents who are regular smokers will eventually die of a smoking-related disease.

People need to take their own role in health and health care seriously, according to Approach Two. We need to make sure that responsibility and accountability go with the individual's right to collaborate on decisions about their health. People should act responsibly to take care of their own health and have the right to appeal decisions by insurers that adversely affect them.

Care for All, Not Just for Some

Getty Images

The city of Chicago & Blue Cross' Carevan travels to Chicago neighborhoods to offer child immunizations during the city's "Free Shots for Tots" program.

In Buffalo, brother and sister George and Tina were both diabetic and both dead before age 25, because they could not regularly afford insulin. It quickly led to other complications. "I see stories like these every day," said the doctor who treated them at a public health clinic, "but the public never hears them because they're anecdotal. The cause of death says kidney failure, but they really died from lack of insurance."

Nearly everyone in the United States has access to some kind of health care. At issue is the kind of care people get, when they get it, and at what cost. "The health care system is set up for people who have cars, who have jobs, who have money, who have education, who know how to speak the same language," says a New Mexico social worker. "We take so much for granted."

But it's not just poor and uninsured people who are falling through the cracks. Nearly all senior citizens are covered by Medicare, but they still don't have coverage for their medications unless they can afford to buy supplemental insurance. Plenty of families who have health insurance still face big bills for eyeglasses and dental care not covered by their policies.

Simply getting to a physician is a challenge to many, whether they have insurance or not. "The health care system expects us to get sick between 9 a.m. and 5 p.m., Monday through Friday," says a working mother, who ends up taking her kids to the emergency room when she can't get time off from her job.

According to Approach Three, the best way to improve health care is to set new priorities to assure that all people get the care they need when they need it. We need to recognize the health care crisis as just that — a devastating problem for large portions of our population. We need to make an unflagging commitment to providing the medical treatment that each person needs. This means expanding health coverage, making health plans more comprehensive, making services more accessible, and reducing racial and gender disparities.

> "The health care system expects us to get sick between 9 a.m. and 5 p.m., Monday through Friday."

Expanded health coverage

"I lived with asthma, probably for years, and suffered because I didn't know where to go and I was absolutely petrified to go to a hospital and accumulate any more bills," says an uninsured Michigan mother. "So I just suffered. Lost time from work, probably didn't get enough time with my children because I was ill."

She eventually found low-cost help, but at a price that was more than financial. "I felt very uncomfortable going to a hospital and expecting health care when I had nothing," she remembers. "You're made to feel like you don't really count. You lose your dignity."

One in seven Americans lacks the basic financial access to care that health insurance provides. Although the numbers of uninsured people dipped slightly in 1999 and 2000, the trend over the last 25 years has been a growing uninsured population.

Recent immigrants fare poorly when it comes to health coverage. Low-income noncitizens are twice as likely to be uninsured as low-income citizens. They are more likely to be employed in jobs without health insurance and less likely to be eligible for public coverage. The welfare reform legislation of the mid-1990s added a new restriction that immigrants must wait five years before they are eligible for Medicaid, even though most of the 30 million foreign-born residents of the U.S. are here legally.

"I do not feel right," says a legal immigrant, who has insurance for only himself through his employer, while his wife and child have no health coverage. "What good is it if I am the only one to get health benefits? Your family should get it first and then yourself. That's what I don't understand."

According to Approach Three, we need a system in which all people have some kind of health coverage that enables them to get timely, appropriate, and often less-costly care. Some say we should accomplish this goal by expanding current government health programs and providing tax incentives to employers who provide adequate coverage to employees.

Others say we should reach the goal of universal coverage by revamping the way health care is financed in this country — by creating a system in which the federal government would be the primary insurer of all Americans, with private, supplemental policies available to those who want and can afford them.

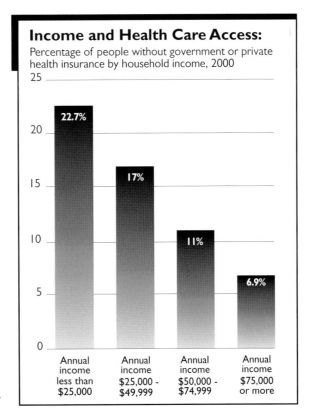

Income and Health Care Access:
Percentage of people without government or private health insurance by household income, 2000

- Annual income less than $25,000: 22.7%
- Annual income $25,000 - $49,999: 17%
- Annual income $50,000 - $74,999: 11%
- Annual income $75,000 or more: 6.9%

Source: "Health Insurance Coverage: 2000," September 2001, U.S. Census Bureau

What Can Be Done

- Clinics could offer more flexible hours and use mobile units to provide health care services in underserved areas.

- Communities could strengthen incentives for doctors to work long term in underserved rural and urban areas.

- Medicaid and CHIP could be expanded to allow citizens to purchase coverage if they earn too much to qualify for free coverage.

- Health agencies could oversee services to ensure unbiased treatment of females, minorities, and the uninsured.

- Governments could provide tax credits to employers who offer comprehensive health insurance, including mental health, dental, and optical care.

- Community volunteers could provide transportation and deliver prescriptions, and health providers could donate health services to those in need.

- Medicare could be expanded to provide low-cost prescription drugs to senior citizens.

- Legislators could create a system that uses tax dollars to provide health coverage for all Americans.

More comprehensive care

"The current system is intolerable," says a physician's wife. "My husband can't treat many of his patients because they can't afford the medications."

Even people who have insurance often worry about having access to care they view as essential to their health. More than a quarter of people on Medicare have no prescription drug coverage. They face the added disadvantage of rapidly rising prescription costs, which more than doubled from $22.06 in 1990 to $45.79 in 2000.

Mental health coverage is limited under many health plans, even though failure to provide adequate outpatient mental health services often results in more expensive inpatient care for people with serious mental illness.

"Even if I needed counseling, my insurance company would only allow a certain number of visits," says a social worker in New Mexico. "When you're chronically mentally ill, you need it all the time. You need supportive services in order to stay out of hospitals and other institutions, like jails. Unfortunately, the jails have become a place where so many acutely mentally ill people are, and that's so tragic."

A community outreach worker advises a mother in El Paso, Texas, on her options for health care for her children under the Children's Health Insurance Program.

Getty Images

Other services, such as dental and vision care, are often treated as extras by their health plans. "When we talk about our cardiac health, no one would say let's make that an option," says a Michigan hospital administrator. "It's visible. There's a lot of information and constant advertising about cardiac health and cardiac centers. Oral health is a more hidden issue, but it's part of a holistic way of being healthy."

Health plans will not be efficient or effective unless they cover the "whole person," according to Approach Three. We need to make sure that health plans cover services that are essential to good health. This includes better coverage of mental health, prescription drugs, and alternative forms of medicine that are found to be effective.

Greater access to care

"It's really hard for some families to get to health services," says one nurse. "Can you imagine a woman at the bus stop with two little ones and a stroller, trying to get on and off the bus? It's really hard for them. The bus system here is really poor. If they just missed the bus they'll have to sit there for an hour."

People's access to health care is affected by where they live. Having health insurance is of limited value to people who live in communities where there is a shortage of health services, particularly if the residents lack cars or public transportation. A recent federal study found that people who live in suburban areas fare significantly better on many key health measures than those who live in the most rural and the most urban parts of the country. This, in part, is also related to the availability of health providers in those areas.

The federal government has identified nearly 3,000 locations across the country that have health care professional shortages in primary care, defined as less than one primary care physician for every 3,500 people. In general, the shortage of health providers is more severe in rural areas, but many inner cities also have problems recruiting and keeping doctors, dentists, nurses, and other health care professionals.

Geographic problems are often compounded by health care provider office hours that are limited to those times when most people are working. Even people with health insurance and a regular doctor can end up using emergency rooms or urgent care centers because they can't afford to take time off from work.

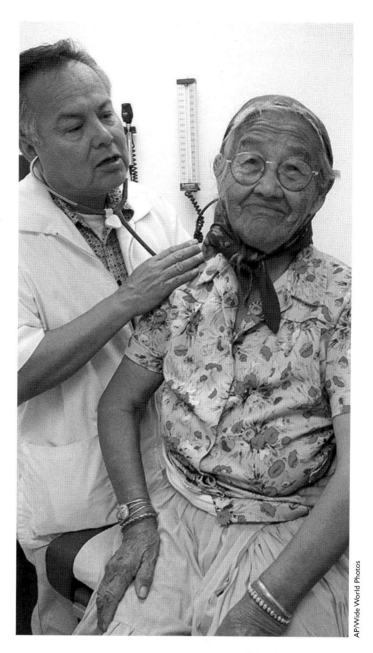

AP/Wide World Photos

A physician assistant examines an elderly patient on the Navajo Indian Reservation near Bluff, Utah. A recent report to Congress found that the nation's oldest American Indians are sicker than other older Americans and generally don't live as long.

Physical barriers to health care can and must be overcome, according to Approach Three. This means taking health services to places where they are not available and making the hours for existing clinics and doctors' offices more flexible.

Racial and gender disparities

Members of racial and ethnic minorities have poorer health status overall. (Part of the disparity is due to less access to care because they are primarily in lower-paying jobs that typically do not offer health insurance.) The chances of being uninsured are almost twice as high for blacks and three times as high for Hispanics than they are for whites.

What Costs and Tradeoffs Should We Be Prepared to Accept ?

A Likely Tradeoff

- This approach will divert funding from other public services or will require Americans to pay more in taxes or insurance premiums.

Concerns about This Approach

- Providing care to everyone will overwhelm the health care system, causing shortages, rationing, and long waits.
- Providing free services limits self-sufficiency and creates dependency.
- Increased governmental involvement will detract from health care services, better provided by the private sector.
- Expanding publicly funded health care forces taxpayers to pay even more for the health care of others.

But access problems for minorities are more than economic. An Institute of Medicine report concluded that "although it is reasonable to assume that the vast majority of health care providers find prejudice morally abhorrent, several studies show that well-meaning people who are not overtly biased or prejudiced typically demonstrate unconscious racial attitudes and stereotypes."

One study, for instance, examined racial disparities in kidney transplants among blacks and whites with end-stage renal disease. The researchers reported that blacks were less than half as likely as whites to be rated as appropriate candidates for kidney transplants. Among those considered as appropriate candidates, blacks received transplants only one-third as often as whites.

Disparities also exist between men's and women's health. For most of medical history, little attention was paid to the differences in women's health beyond reproduction. Researchers studied male subjects almost exclusively and assumed that their findings applied equally to women. But in the case of heart attacks, for instance, women often have different symptoms than the classic chest pains, and their early signs are often misdiagnosed and go untreated.

Considerable advances have been made in women's health during the past two decades, but barriers to equal care for the sexes still exist, according to a recent report by the Institute of Medicine. "Sex does matter," says Dr. Mary-Lou Perdue, who chaired the committee that wrote the report. "It matters in ways that we did not expect. Undoubtedly, it also matters in ways that we have not begun to imagine."

Whether intentional or not, differences in care based on race and gender persist, according to this approach. This means rectifying the disparities that exist through better education, outreach, research, clinical practices, and laws.

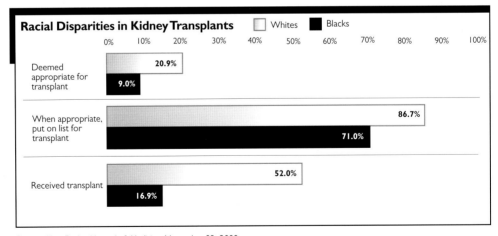

Source: *New England Journal of Medicine*, November 23, 2000

Learn More about Health Care in America

These organizations are among many throughout the country that provide information on a wide range of issues that impact health and health care.

Private Foundations and Nonprofit Organizations

Alliance for Health Reform, a nonpartisan organization chaired by Senator Jay Rockefeller and Senator Bill Frist, provides information about different perspectives on the nation's health care problems and tradeoffs posed by competing proposals for change. Web site: www.allhealth.org. Phone: (202) 789-2300.

The American Medical Association develops and promotes standards in medical practice, research, and education; advocates on behalf of patients and physicians; and provides information on matters important to the health of America. Web site: www.ama-assn.org. Phone: (312) 464-5000.

The Commonwealth Fund is a private foundation that supports independent research on health and social issues. It publishes a wide range of reports on health and health care issues, which can be ordered on-line or by phone. Web site: www.cmwf.org. Phone: (212) 606-3800.

Healthwise, Inc. is a nonprofit organization of health professionals dedicated to helping people do a better job of staying healthy and taking care of their health problems. They publish easy-to-use guides for health consumers. Web site: www.healthwise.org. Toll-free phone: 1-800-706-9646.

The Robert Wood Johnson Foundation is the largest U.S. foundation devoted to improving health and health care for all Americans. It makes grants and publishes reports on health care access, care for chronic conditions, and healthy lifestyles. Web site: www.rwjf.org. Toll-free phone: 1-888-631-9989.

The Kaiser Family Foundation is an independent, national health philanthropic organization dedicated to providing information and analysis on health issues to policymakers, the media, and the general public. Web site: www.kff.org. Toll-free number to order publications: 1-800-656-4533.

The Community Voices Initiative of the W.K. Kellogg Foundation is a national initiative to improve health care for the underserved. It supports 13 local projects in 11 states and offers a variety of free publications. Web site: www.wkkf.org. Phone: (616) 968-0413.

The Institute of Medicine is part of the National Academy of Science, a private, nonprofit society of distinguished scholars. The institute provides objective, timely, authoritative information and advice on human health to government, the corporate sector, the professions, and the public. Web site: www.iom.edu. Order publications toll-free at 1-888-624-8373.

Government Agencies

The Centers on Disease Control and Prevention (CDC) is recognized as the lead federal agency for protecting people's health and safety and providing credible information on a wide variety of health-related topics. Web site: www.cdc.gov. Toll-free phone: 1-800-311-3435.

The Office of Minority Health in the federal Department of Health and Human Resources works to improve the health of racial and ethnic populations through the development of effective policies and programs that help eliminate disparities in health. Web site: www.omhrc.gov. Toll-free phone: 1-800-444-6472.

The National Institutes of Health (NIH) is the federal focal point for medical research in the United States, supporting research in its own laboratories and in universities and hospitals across the country. NIH includes many diverse institutes and programs, including the Office of Research on Women's Health and the National Center on Minority Health and Health Disparities. Web site: www.nih.gov. Phone: (301) 496-4000.

Comparing Approaches

Health care is a profoundly personal experience that has immense public consequences. The care we get — or don't get — affects our ability to lead long and healthy lives. It has ripple effects throughout our society, influencing children's ability to succeed in school, the productivity of American workers, and the lifestyles of our aging population. From patients to politicians, from doctors to insurance executives, an overwhelming number of Americans say we desperately need to reform health care in this country. Careful thought and deliberation are needed to understand the nature of the problems in health care and to consider possible courses of action. Although they are not mutually exclusive, the approaches outlined on these pages reflect different perspectives and priorities that people bring to this critical issue.

Approach One: Connected Parts, Not Fragmented Pieces

The most effective way to improve health care in America is to take firm hold of it and make it run like a true, well-coordinated system. We need to take the existing, unwieldy collection of health care fragments and fashion them into a connected web of health care services, where information flows readily between the pieces and they work in concert. This is the best way to curb costs and provide health care in a timely way.

What Can Be Done?

- Citizens and professionals could serve on health care councils that coordinate the use of facilities and medical services within a region.
- Health care providers could develop systems to share patient information and coordinate care.
- Patients could make sure their doctors are aware of treatments from other doctors and could carry a "health passport" card containing their medical history.
- Insurers could set guidelines to reduce unnecessary medical tests, and medical schools could educate physicians to use costly procedures efficiently.
- Legislators could enact laws to increase the monitoring of health care billing practices and stiffen penalties for fraud.
- Congress could establish a nationwide mandatory reporting system to monitor and learn from medical errors.
- Hospitals could limit the use of emergency rooms to emergency care only.
- Legislators could set caps on awards for medical lawsuits.

A Likely Tradeoff?

- This approach uses scarce health care resources to develop systems for coordinating medical care rather than providing direct care to patients.

Concerns about This Approach

- Increased legislation adds extra layers to a health care system already choked by bureaucracy.
- Making personal medical records more available makes personal privacy more vulnerable.
- Limiting malpractice awards constrains citizens' rights for appropriate compensation.
- Focusing on medical errors casts doubt on the vast majority of medical professionals who are highly skilled and competent.

Approach Two: Partners, Not Just Patients

We need to create new relationships in health care where consumers and professionals work hand in hand, with patients becoming partners in their health care. We need to take time to communicate, to help people make informed decisions, and to educate about healthy lifestyles. This is the best way to improve the health of Americans and to lay a firm foundation for personal responsibility and prevention that will result in long-term savings.

What Can Be Done?

- Insurers and health care administrators could support more face-to-face time between doctors and patients.
- Medical school training could focus on doctor-patient collaboration and "patient-centered care."
- Media and schools could provide more information about health risks, such as smoking and obesity.
- Citizens could serve on medical licensing, review, and health assistance boards.
- Employers could involve employees in decisions about health plans, benefits, and costs.
- Individuals could take more responsibility for practicing healthy habits and preventive health care.
- Insurers could charge higher premiums to customers who engage in risky health habits.
- Legislators could pass laws to protect patients' rights to appeal decisions by insurers.
- Community groups could provide health education and opportunities to discuss public health care policies.

A Likely Tradeoff?

- This approach depends on the time-consuming work of changing relationships and personal habits rather than addressing existing gaps in health coverage.

Concerns about This Approach

- Many people will not be willing or able to be so involved in learning about their illnesses and treatments.
- Demands for physicians' and nurses' time will strain a system that is already stretched too thin.
- Doctors should focus on practicing effective clinical treatments, not developing personal relationships.
- Shared decision making confuses who is responsible for medical decisions and treatment.

Approach Three: Care for All, Not Just for Some

We need to set new priorities in health care aimed at providing Americans the care they need when they need it. We need to seal up the cracks in the system so that people don't fall through. We need an unflagging commitment providing the medical treatment that each person needs. This is the best way to improve individual health and prevent illnesses that are more difficult and expensive to treat.

What Can Be Done?

- Clinics could offer more flexible hours and use mobile units to provide health care services in underserved areas.
- Communities could strengthen incentives for doctors to work long-term in underserved rural and urban areas.
- Medicaid and CHIP could be expanded to allow citizens to purchase coverage if they earn too much to qualify for free coverage.
- Health agencies could oversee services to ensure unbiased treatment of females, minorities, and the uninsured.
- Governments could provide tax credits to employers who offer comprehensive health insurance, including mental health, dental, and optical care.
- Community volunteers could provide transportation and deliver prescriptions, and health providers could donate health services to those in need.
- Medicare could be expanded to provide low-cost prescription drugs to senior citizens.
- Legislators could create a system that uses tax dollars to provide health coverage for all Americans.

A Likely Tradeoff?

- This approach will divert funding from other public services or will require Americans to pay more in taxes or insurance premiums.

Concerns about This Approach

- Providing care to everyone will overwhelm the health care system, causing shortages, rationing, and long waits.
- Providing free services limits self-sufficiency and creates dependency.
- Increased governmental involvement will detract from health care services better provided by the private sector.
- Expanding publicly funded health care forces taxpayers to pay even more for the health care of others.

What Are the National Issues Forums?

National Issues Forums bring together citizens around the nation to discuss challenging social and political issues of the day. They have addressed issues such as the economy, education, healthcare, foreign affairs, poverty, and crime.

Thousands of civic, service, and religious organizations, as well as libraries, high schools, and colleges, have sponsored forums. The sponsoring organizations select topics from among each year's most pressing public concerns, then design and coordinate their own forum programs, which are held through the fall, winter, and spring.

A different kind of talk

No two forums are alike. They range from small study circles to large gatherings modeled after town meetings, but all are different from everyday conversations and adversarial debates.

Since forums seek to increase understanding of complicated issues, participants need not start out with detailed knowledge of an issue. Forum organizers distribute issue books such as this one, featuring a nonpartisan overview of an issue and a choice of several public responses. By presenting each issue in a nonpartisan way, forums encourage participants to take a fresh look at the issues and at their own convictions.

In the forums, participants share their opinions, their concerns, and their knowledge. With the help of moderators and the issue books, participants weigh several possible ways for society to address a problem. They analyze each choice, the arguments for and against it, and the tradeoffs and other implications of the choice. Moderators encourage participants, as they gravitate to one option or another, to examine their basic values as individuals and as community members.

The search for common ground

Forums enrich participants' thinking on public issues. Participants confront each issue head-on, make an informed decision about how to address it, and come to terms with the likely consequences of their choices. In this deliberative process, participants often accept choices that are not entirely consistent with their individual wishes and that impose costs they had not initially considered. This happens because the forum process helps people see issues from different points of view; participants use discussion to discover, not persuade or advocate. The best deliberative forums can help participants move toward shared, stable, well-informed public judgments about important issues.

Participants may hold sharply different opinions and beliefs, but in the forums they discuss their attitudes, concerns, and convictions about each issue and, as a group, seek to resolve their conflicting priorities and principles. In this way, participants move from making individual choices to making choices as members of a community — the kinds of choices from which public action may result.

Building community through public deliberation

In a democracy, citizens must come together to find answers they can all live with — while acknowledging that individuals have differing opinions. Forums help people find the areas where their interests and goals overlap. This allows a public voice to emerge that can give direction to public policy.

The forums are nonpartisan and do not advocate a particular solution to any public issue, nor should they be confused with referenda or public opinion polls. Rather, the forums enable diverse groups of Americans to determine together what direction they want policy to take, what kinds of action and legislation they favor and what, for their common good, they oppose.

Moving to action

Forums can lead to several kinds of public action. Generally, a public voice emerges in the results of the forums, and that helps set the government's compass, since forum results are shared with elected officials each year. Also, as a result of attending forums, individuals and groups may decide individually or with others to help remedy a public problem through citizen actions outside of government.

How to start a forum

Forums are initiated at the local level by civic and educational organizations. For information about starting a forum and using our materials, write the NIF Institute, P.O. Box 75306, Washington, D.C. 20013-5306, or phone 800-433-7834. On the Internet: http://www.nifi.org.

NATIONAL ISSUES FORUMS

Examining Health Care
What's the Public's Prescription?

Now that you've had the chance to participate in a forum on this issue, please complete this questionnaire. Your opinions, along with those of others who participate in these forums, will be reflected in a national summary report. The report will be available to all, including those who take part in the forums, officeholders, and the news media.

1. Do you agree or disagree with the statements below?

	Strongly agree	Somewhat agree	Somewhat disagree	Strongly disagree	Not sure
a. All Americans should have some kind of health insurance.	☐	☐	☐	☐	☐
b. Doctors should treat patients as full partners in their own health care.	☐	☐	☐	☐	☐
c. Huge malpractice awards are driving up the cost of health care.	☐	☐	☐	☐	☐
d. Regardless of income, minorities do not receive the same quality of health care as whites do.	☐	☐	☐	☐	☐
e. The public should have easier access to information about doctors' mistakes.	☐	☐	☐	☐	☐
f. Patients dealing with many parts of the health care system often have no one to oversee the whole picture.	☐	☐	☐	☐	☐

2. Do you favor or oppose each of these actions?

	Strongly favor	Somewhat favor	Somewhat oppose	Strongly oppose	Not sure
a. Expand Medicare to include prescription drugs.	☐	☐	☐	☐	☐
b. Require doctors to be retested periodically, to ensure that they are still competent.	☐	☐	☐	☐	☐
c. Make people whose choice of behavior threatens their own health, pay more for insurance.	☐	☐	☐	☐	☐
d. Set caps on awards for medical lawsuits.	☐	☐	☐	☐	☐
e. Provide health care to all Americans through a government-funded system.	☐	☐	☐	☐	☐
f. Create local and regional health care systems to make doctors and hospitals share services and equipment.	☐	☐	☐	☐	☐

3. Do you favor or oppose the statements listed below?

	Strongly favor	Somewhat favor	Somewhat oppose	Strongly oppose	Not sure
a. Health care providers should coordinate and share facilities and resources, EVEN IF patients would have to wait longer for some services.	☐	☐	☐	☐	☐
b. Doctors should spend more time with their patients, EVEN IF this raises the cost of health care.	☐	☐	☐	☐	☐
c. All Americans should have access to basic health care services, EVEN IF this means cutting coverage of some costly treatments.	☐	☐	☐	☐	☐

4. Are you thinking differently about this issue now that you have participated in the forum?

☐ Yes   ☐ No

If yes, how?

_____

_____

_____

_____

5. In your forum, did you talk about aspects of the issue you hadn't considered before?

☐ Yes   ☐ No

6. What, if anything, might citizens in your community do differently as a result of this forum?

_____

_____

_____

_____

7. How many National Issues Forums have you attended, including this one?

☐ 1–3   ☐ 4–6   ☐ 7 or more   ☐ Not sure

8. Are you male or female?   ☐ Male   ☐ Female

9. Are you:

☐ African American   ☐ Asian American   ☐ Hispanic   ☐ Native American   ☐ White/Caucasian

☐ Other (please specify) _____

10. How old are you?

☐ 17 or younger   ☐ 18–30   ☐ 31–45   ☐ 46–64   ☐ 65 or older

11. Where do you live?

☐ Rural   ☐ Small Town   ☐ Large City   ☐ Suburban

12. Who pays for your health insurance?

☐ Your employer   ☐ Medicare   ☐ Medicaid   ☐ You   ☐ I have no health insurance.

13. What is your ZIP code?   _____

Please give this form to the forum leader, or mail it to National Issues Forums Research, 100 Commons Road, Dayton, Ohio, 45459-2777.